A Fabric Lover's Dilemma

We love our fabrics, don't we? We loved them when we bought them, we loved them when we cut into them, and we loved them when we made them into those lovely quilts. We love every little scrap leftover from countless projects. Little gems of color, our scraps sparkle and dance. How can we part with them?

If you find it hard to part with every last scrap of fabric, then this book is for you. Read on to find solutions for your scrap-saving mania (that's what people call it anyway). Learn to tackle and control your scrap pile. Find new ways to creatively put those small pieces to use. Thirteen easy-to-create patterns will use up those beautiful scraps that have begun to pile up.

DON'T THROW THAT AWAY!

For countless years I have recycled our newspapers, glass and aluminum cans. So is it any wonder I couldn't throw my fabric scraps away? My scraps were becoming an issue with me. They had a tendency to spill out of cupboard doors, kept boxes from closing and made little paths that followed me from room to room. I began to think something should be done.

Looking at my scraps, I thought about what patterns I could use and what size scraps would be manageable to handle. I found out that I am a serious scrap saver, which means I can allow myself to save very small scraps (and use them). I like to save anything that is at least 1" x 1" (I don't use a great amount of these tiny squares, but they have a real use at times). Having learned this about myself, I gave myself permission to throw out any scraps that were too small. This is a great relief. I no longer have to look at each little scrap and debate whether to keep it or not. If it is too small, I can toss it without a guilty conscience. If you are a serious scrap saver, then you can proceed and use this book with ease.

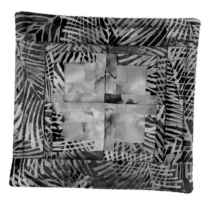

5¾" square coaster from project scraps

If you think people who save 1" scraps are crazy, then you may be just a scrap saver, which is fine. You need to determine what is the smallest-size scrap that you would use in a pattern. Maybe it is 2" x 2" or 3" x 3". You can certainly use the patterns included in this book, but you will need to enlarge them to suit your scrap sizes.

The following is a list of what you should save:

• Any scraps at least 1" across to allow for ¼" seams on each side.

• Any leftover strips from bindings and sashings.

• Triangles and corner scraps from other projects. So many patterns now call for using squares, sewing on the diagonal and trimming off the corners. Save those little corners! You will impress your friends with all your teeny-tiny triangles.

Scrap of Information

Fabric pieces that are larger than 3" x 3" I consider to be chunks—perfectly good pieces of fabric that can stay in your regular stash—or square them up and set them aside in a box for 4", 5" or 6" blocks. These can later be used for fabric block exchanges, and the great thing is they are already cut to size.

SO YOU HAVE A BUNCH OF SCRAPS, NOW WHAT?

Where to Store Your Scraps

Start with a designated scrap box where you can toss your scraps. Keep the box handy near your sewing area. These scraps may get rumpled and jumbled and wrinkled and frayed after you've fumbled through the box a few times. Don't be dismayed—this may just mean you need another scrap box.

I now have a set of medium-sized plastic drawers that sits beside my machine, and when I create a new scrap, I just pop it in a drawer for future use. The drawers are not deep, so it isn't necessary to do a lot of messing around to find scraps. This is a neat way to store scraps until you want to use them. I find that when my drawers don't close anymore, it is time to get busy and make more scrappy blocks.

Sort the Scraps by Color

I find it very helpful to sort the scraps by color. I have a drawer for reds and greens, one for whites, blacks and browns, one for blues (I tend to have a lot of blue scraps), one for purples and brights, and one or two drawers just for miscellaneous scraps. See what suits you best. You may use a lot of green fabrics in your quilting, so you may have more green scraps than anything else. It is interesting to see what grows

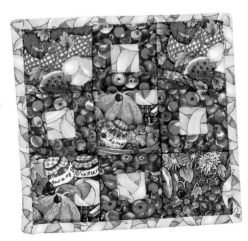

5¾" square coaster from project scraps

from your scrap piles. I sometimes have a feeling that they are multiplying in my drawers.

What Patterns to Use?

What patterns can you use with your little scraps? Little patterns, of course! These little scraps are great for paper-piecing patterns. Little pieces in these blocks are easy to sew and require no precision cutting, and there is no stretching of bias fabrics. You can use any kind of fabric scrap with paper-pieced patterns.

The patterns in this book are very easy to complete in a short amount of time and require little concentration. They use up scraps quickly.

PAPER-PIECING INSTRUCTIONS

If you have a home copier, you can print your own patterns. It is fine to print them on regular copy paper. There are some specialty sheets available that are thinner and easier to tear. If you want to try them out, check your local shops to see what is available.

Follow these general instructions for successful paper piecing.

1. Cut out all patterns along the outside lines.

2. All seams are sewn with a small stitch length. These tight stitches allow you to easily tear off the paper from the back of the block when the project is completed.

3. Always start and stop sewing several stitches beyond the marked lines.

4. When joining two paper-pieced blocks in a project, sew the blocks together along the seam line; then tear off the ¼" paper along the seams and press the blocks. This will relieve bulk in the seam areas.

5. Take a scrap of fabric approximately ½" larger than space 1 and place it right side up on the unmarked side of the paper pattern so that the fabric completely covers space 1 and extends approximately ¼" beyond the lines as shown in Figure 1. **Note:** *Hold the pattern up to the light with the numbers facing you and see if the fabric extends beyond all the lines of space 1.* Pin in place.

Figure 1

6. Turn the paper marked side up and fold on the line between spaces 1 and 2 as shown in Figure 2; trim the fabric about ¼" from the folded edges.

Figure 2

7. Select a scrap of fabric approximately ½" larger than space 2.

8. Align fabric 2 with the edge of the trimmed fabric with right sides together.

9. Hold the edges of the fabrics with your fingers and fold the fabric over to check that it covers space 2 as shown in Figure 3.

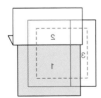

Figure 3

10. Lay the paper and fabric flat again; sew on the line between spaces 1 and 2.

11. Finger-press piece 2 flat.

12. Turn the paper side up; fold on the line between spaces 2 and 3.

13. Carefully pull the paper from the threads that extend beyond the lines; trim the fabric about ¼" from the folded edge as shown in Figure 4.

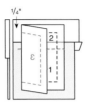

Figure 4

14. Select a scrap of fabric approximately ½" larger than space 3.

15. Align this piece right sides together with piece 2 along the seam line; fold back, checking that piece 3 will completely cover space 3 with fabric extending beyond all lines.

16. Turn the pattern over and sew along the line between spaces 2 and 3 from one edge of the pattern to the other as shown in Figure 5.

Figure 5

17. Press the completed block; trim excess fabric around the outside edge of the pattern to complete the unit.

18. Do not remove paper backing until directed to do so in the individual patterns.

Scrap of Information
Make a mistake in your piecing? Don't want to take out those little stitches? It's OK, just toss it out. It's just a scrap, remember?

COLORS IN SCRAP-SAVER QUILTS

Scrap-saver quilts can be made in a variety of color arrangements. Here are some tips on possible colorations.

Two-Color Quilts

Using two colors in your quilt is a great scrap-saver usage. Choose two colors that look good together and gather all the scraps you have in those two colors. The variety of shades and hues in the two colors will give an added element to your quilt. (See Sweet Pea on page 24 and Blue Illusions Table Runner on page 33.)

Scrappy Quilts

These quilts can be made using any scraps you have without thought to matching any colors. (See Striped Squares Candle Mat on page 18 and Pineapple Welcome on page 42.)

Planned Scrappy Quilts

Planned scrappy quilts are quilts that start with a group of colors and use all the scraps you have in those colors. (See Floral Trellis Quilt on page 27, Mini Logs Wall Quilt on page 39 and Christmas Squares Table Mat on page 46.)

Charm Quilts

It is possible to make charm quilts with little scraps, but this requires planning to be sure that each fabric is used only once. My personal goal is to use up as many fabric scraps as possible, not to keep each scrap accounted for; so I have not included an example of a charm quilt. If this is what you like to do, it would make a great memory quilt of all your past projects. Go for it!

Scrap of Information

Scraps of large prints are usable in scrap-saver quilts, just remember the pieces in the block patterns are small and only one color may show up from a large-scale print fabric.

3¾" square coaster from project scraps

One word of caution in selecting color combinations for your patterns. Be aware that you need to have strong contrast between your light, medium and dark fabrics or your design will fade out and not be visible.

Some patterns are suited to having one fabric color for background. Using the same fabric, or a variety of fabrics very close in color, is soothing to the eye and will liven up the scrappy areas of the project. (See Bow Tie Place Mat, page 21 and Stick Pinwheels Place Mat, page 36.)

THE SCRAP SAVER'S DILEMMA: TO ADD OR NOT TO ADD FABRIC FROM YOUR STASH

The dilemma for the serious scrap saver is whether or not to use a non-scrap in a project. For any other person, this is not a problem, but the serious scrap saver delights in finding treasures in her scrap pile. Here is my answer: Go ahead! Does it really matter? Would anyone else know you snuck a non-scrap into your project?

Sometimes you may need a special spark of color not available in your stash of scraps at the moment. Or, you may want a background color that requires more fabric than your scrap stash has of one particular color field. The thing no serious scrap saver would do is to go out and purchase fabric for her project!

Go ahead and allow yourself to take some snips from fabrics in your regular stash if you want. Those chunks of fabric in your stash may someday end up in your scrap boxes anyway.

Your regular fabric stash is a great place to shop for sashing strips and border fabrics for your small quilts. This works out great and also enlarges your quilts in a hurry.

Go to it and attack that stash!

QUILT SIZES

You will be able to make a wonderful rainbow of miniature quilts, hot pads, table mats, place mats, table runners and coasters using the patterns in this book. By using up your scraps you can make beautiful things for yourself and for gifts. People will marvel at the tiny gems you've created and will think you've worked for hours. And you can tell them you made them with scraps.

Scrap of Information
Create hot pads and coasters by using several paper-pieced blocks and adding borders and sashings to enlarge them to the size you prefer.

SCRAPPY BORDERS

Scraps can also be used in borders. Think about piecing scraps together into strips for sashings or borders as in Floral Trellis Quilt on page 27.

Foundation patterns can be repeated in the border as in Auntie's Flower Garden on page 7.

Get creative! The borders can add an extra spark to those little blocks.

HEY, HEY, LET'S APPLIQUÉ

Do you have any leftover scraps of fusible webbing? Use those pieces or a new piece, if you must, to fuse fabric scraps for use in appliqué. Use your imagination to create appliqué borders using scraps as in Mini Logs Wall Quilt on page 39 or Pineapple Welcome on page 42.

Don't forget that buttons, charms and beads can be used for embellishments to add interest to your scrap quilts.

QUILTING

Very little quilting is needed for small quilts. The quilts in this book have small pieced blocks with many seams that make hand quilting difficult.

With the variety of fabric prints in the pieced blocks, the quilting will not show up well, so hand quilting is not necessary or recommended. Machine-quilt mainly in the ditch around the blocks and save hand-quilted designs for larger border strips and other open areas.

THREAD

The piecing in each block is done using a very small stitch length. Machine stitches should not show, making it possible to use up those bobbins that have a little bit of thread left on them.

After you've used up your miscellaneous bobbins, I recommend using a gray or dark gray neutral-color thread for most paper piecing. The color blends in well with most projects and saves changing thread for each scrap.

When quilting most projects, I recommend a clear monofilament thread around the pieced blocks. Matching or contrasting threads are better suited for the wider borders. Do not use monofilament thread for hot pads because it could melt when exposed to heat.

BATTING

If you are a scrap saver, I know you save those larger pieces of batting left over from your quilts. Now is the time to use them. Thin batting is a must for small projects. For hot pads, be sure to use two or three layers of 100 percent cotton batting.

6¼" square coaster from project scraps

STARTING YOUR PROJECT

You have collected, sorted and stored your scraps. You have selected a pattern. Now, pull out your scraps and check to see if you have enough of the colors you have chosen to use. This will be a guess at this point, but you should have at least a small pile of each color to get started. If you are not sure if you have enough scraps for your project, try one of the following:

• Go through your regular stash to find colors that might work with your scrap piles.

• Let your scrap-saver friends know you are looking for scraps. They will be happy to give you whatever they have that is smaller than they normally save. It will make them feel like they are helping you and not being wasteful.

FINISHING YOUR QUILT

Use the following instructions as a guide for finishing the quilts in this book.

1. If you will be hand-quilting a special quilting design on your quilt top, mark the design as desired using a water-erasable marker or pencil or a chalk pencil.

2. Sandwich the thin batting piece between the completed top and prepared backing piece; pin, baste or spray-baste layers together to hold flat.

3. Quilt as desired using clear monofilament or thread of choice to either blend or contrast with the quilt top.

4. When quilting is complete, remove pins or basting. Remove marked quilting lines if applicable.

5. Trim batting and backing edges even with the quilted top.

6. Join the binding strips with right sides together on short ends with diagonal seams to make one long strip as shown in Figure 6; press seams open. Fold the binding strip with wrong sides together along the length and press.

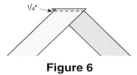

Figure 6

7. Place the binding strip right sides together with the quilted top along the center of one side, matching raw edges. Stitch all around, mitering corners as shown in Figure 7.

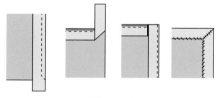

Figure 7

8. Overlap or join strip ends at the beginning/end; press binding strip flat.

9. Turn binding to the back side to enclose seam, hand-stitch in place on the back side, or machine-stitch in the ditch of the binding seam on the top side to catch the binding strip on the back side to finish. ■

Auntie's Flower Garden

Buttons can be used for the flower centers and in the borders to make this scrappy flower garden mini.

PROJECT SPECIFICATIONS
Skill Level: Beginner
Quilt Size: 12½" x 12½"
Block Size: 2½" x 2½"
Number of Blocks: 9

FABRIC & BATTING
- Scraps vintage fabrics
- ⅛ yard green solid
- ¼ yard yellow solid
- Backing 17" x 17"
- Batting 17" x 17"

SUPPLIES & TOOLS
- Neutral color all-purpose thread
- Quilting thread
- 8 each red, green and blue ⅝" buttons
- Basic tools and supplies

Cutting
1. Cut one 1¾" by fabric width strip yellow solid; subcut the strips into two 1¾" x 8" A strips and two 1¾" x 10½" B strips.

2. Cut four 1¾" x 1¾" C squares green solid.

3. Cut two 2¼" by fabric width strips yellow solid for binding.

Piecing the Blocks
1. Prepare 34 copies of the paper-piecing pattern.

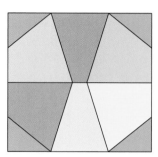

Auntie's Flower Garden
2½" x 2½" Block

2. Referring to Figure 1 and the instructions for Paper Piecing on page 2, complete 34 pieced units using scraps for pieces 1, 2 and 3 and green solid for pieces 4 and 5.

Figure 1

3. Trim paper-pieced units along outer solid line.

4. Join two paper-pieced units to complete one block as shown in Figure 2; press seam open.

Figure 2

Completing the Top
1. Join three blocks to make a row; press seams open.

2. Join rows to complete the pieced center; press seams open.

3. Sew A strips to opposite sides and B strips to the top and bottom of the pieced center; press seams toward A strips.

4. Join four paper-pieced units to make a strip as shown in Figure 3; press seams open. Repeat to make four strips.

Figure 3

5. Sew a pieced strip to opposite sides of the pieced center; press seams toward A strips.

6. Sew C to each end of the remaining pieced strips; press seams toward C.

7. Sew the strips to the top and bottom of the pieced center; press seams toward B strips to complete the top.

8. Remove paper from all pieced units.

Completing the Quilt

1. Complete the quilt using previously cut binding strips referring to Finishing Your Quilt on page 6.

2. Referring to the Placement Diagram and the project photo, sew a button in the center of each block in the quilt center and in the center of each pieced unit in the borders to complete the quilt. ◼

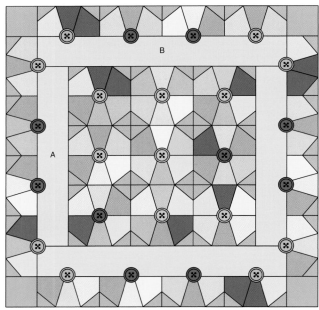

Auntie's Flower Garden
Placement Diagram
12½" x 12½"

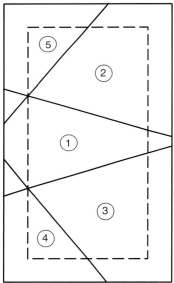

Paper-Piecing Pattern
Make 34 copies

Two-Point Block Quilt

Leftover light solid-color scraps make perfect background pieces in this quilt design filled with tiny star points.

PROJECT SPECIFICATIONS
Skill Level: Intermediate
Quilt Size: 28½" x 28½"
Block Size: 5" x 5"
Number of Blocks: 13

FABRIC & BATTING
- Scraps light, medium and dark prints
- Scraps pastel solids
- ¼ yard binding fabric
- Backing 34" x 34"
- Batting 34" x 34"

SUPPLIES & TOOLS
- Neutral color all-purpose thread
- Quilting thread
- Paper
- Basic tools and supplies

Cutting
1. Prepare templates for pieces A and B using patterns given; cut as directed on each piece.

2. Cut three 2¼" by fabric width strips binding fabric.

Completing the Blocks
1. Make 52 copies of the paper-piecing pattern.

2. Referring to the instructions for Paper Piecing on page 2 and Figure 1, complete four matching-fabric paper-pieced units using pastel solid for pieces 1, 3 and 5, dark scrap for piece 6, light scrap for pieces 2 and 4 and medium scrap for piece 7.

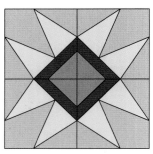

Two-Point
5" x 5" Block

Figure 1   **Figure 2**

3. Join the four matching paper-pieced units as shown in Figure 2 to complete one block; press seams open. Repeat to make 13 blocks.

Completing the Top
1. Arrange the blocks in diagonal rows with A triangles as shown in Figure 3; join in rows. Press seams of adjacent rows in opposite directions.

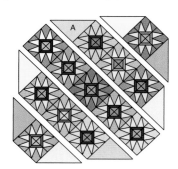

Figure 3

     HOUSE OF WHITE BIRCHES, BERNE, INDIANA 46711   DRGNETWORK.COM

2. Join the rows and add B to corners to complete the pieced center; press seams in one direction.

3. Remove paper pieces.

4. Join five A and two B triangles to make a side strip as shown in Figure 4; press seams toward the side with two A pieces. Repeat to make four side strips.

Figure 4

5. Sew a side strip to opposite sides of the pieced center; press seams toward the side strips.

6. Join two B triangles as shown in Figure 5; press seam in one direction. Repeat to make four B units.

Figure 5

7. Sew a B unit to each end of each remaining side strip to make a B strip as shown in Figure 6; press seams toward the B units.

Figure 6

8. Sew a B strip to the remaining sides of the pieced center to complete the pieced top referring to the Placement Diagram for positioning of strips; press seams toward the B strips.

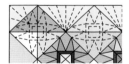
Figure 7

9. Complete the quilt using previously cut binding strips referring to Finishing Your Quilt on page 6. **Note:** *The blocks are machine-quilted in the ditch of seams. The block design is copied and machine-quilted in the joined A triangles between the borders and the pieced top and in the four intersection B triangles in the corners as shown in Figure 7. The outside A triangles are quilted in angled lines radiating from the inner points to the outer edges, as shown in Figure 7.* ■

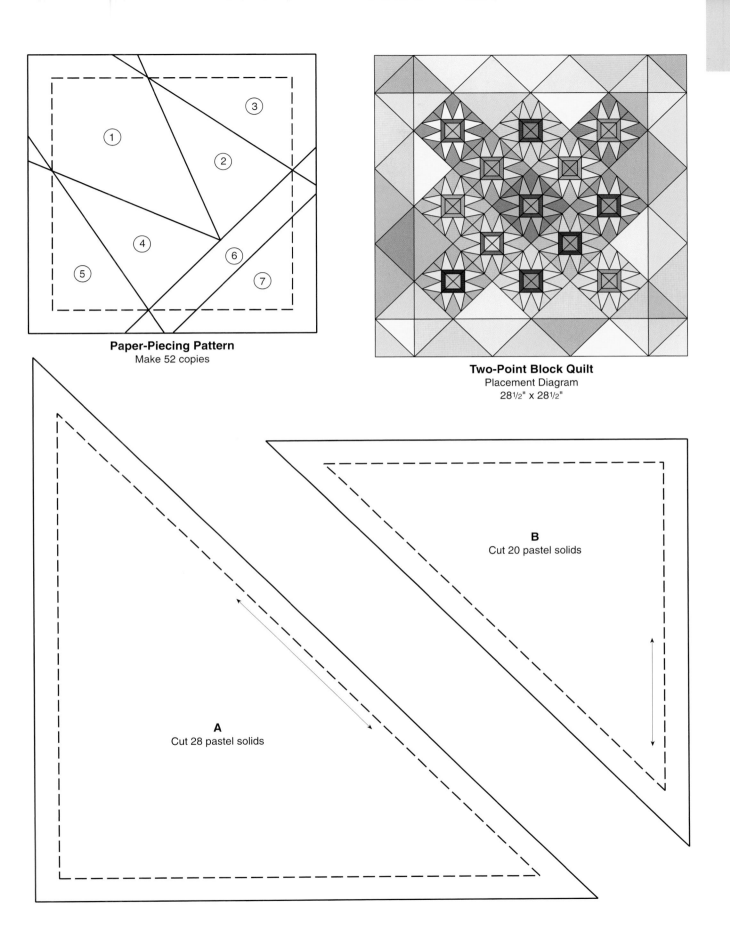

Paper-Piecing Pattern
Make 52 copies

Two-Point Block Quilt
Placement Diagram
28½" x 28½"

A
Cut 28 pastel solids

B
Cut 20 pastel solids

Crazy-Patch Table Topper

One of the oldest methods of using scraps is the crazy-patch method. Blocks may be made on foundations of fabric or paper and with or without patterns. A variety of paper-pieced designs were used in this sashed table topper.

PROJECT SPECIFICATIONS
Skill Level: Beginner
Quilt Size: 16½" x 21"
Block Size: 3" x 3"
Number of Blocks: 6

FABRIC & BATTING
- Scraps jewel-tone fabrics
- ⅛ yard green tonal
- ⅛ yard rose mottled
- ¼ yard blue tonal
- ⅜ yard black solid
- Backing 21" x 25"
- Batting 21" x 25"

SUPPLIES & TOOLS
- Neutral color all-purpose thread
- Quilting thread
- Paper
- Basic tools and supplies

Cutting
1. Cut one 2" by fabric width strip rose mottled; subcut strip into (12) 2" A squares.

2. Cut one 3½" by fabric width strip black solid; subcut strip into (17) 2" B strips.

3. Cut two 3" by fabric width strips blue tonal;

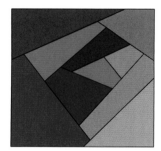

Crazy-Patch
3" x 3" Block

subcut one strip into two 15½" C strips and the remaining strip into two 16" D strips.

4. Cut two 1" by fabric width strips green tonal; subcut one strip into two 20½" E strips and two 17" F strips.

5. Cut three 2¼" by fabric width strips black solid for binding.

Completing the Blocks
1. Make six copies of the paper-piecing patterns in any combination.

2. Referring to the instructions for Paper Piecing on page 2 and Figure 1, complete six paper-pieced Crazy-Patch blocks.

Figure 1

Completing the Topper

1. Join two Crazy-Patch blocks with three B strips to make a block row as shown in Figure 2; press seams toward B strips. Repeat to make three block rows.

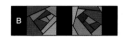

Figure 2

2. Join two B strips with three A squares to make a sashing row as shown in Figure 3; press seams toward A. Repeat to make four sashing rows.

Figure 3

3. Join the sashing rows with the block rows to complete the pieced center; press seams toward the sashing rows.

4. Sew a C strip to opposite long sides and D strips to the top and bottom of the pieced center; press seams toward C and D strips.

5. Sew an E strip to opposite long sides and F strips to the top and bottom of the pieced center; press seams toward E and F strips to complete the pieced top.

6. Remove paper from all paper-pieced blocks.

7. Complete the topper using previously cut binding strips referring to Finishing Your Quilt on page 6. ■

Scrap of Information
Wide borders provide a nice area for hand or machine quilting.

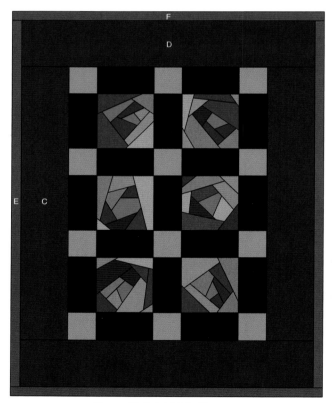

Crazy-Patch Table Topper
Placement Diagram
16½" x 21"

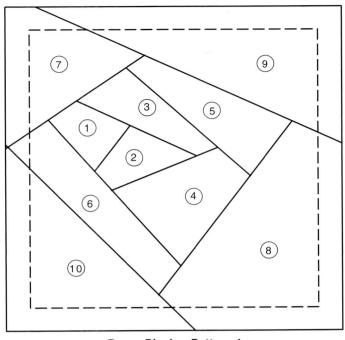

Paper-Piecing Pattern 1

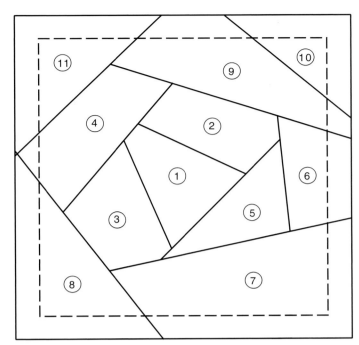

Paper-Piecing Pattern 2

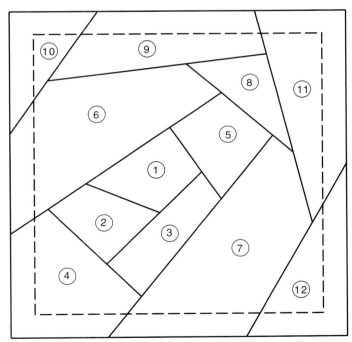

Paper-Piecing Pattern 3

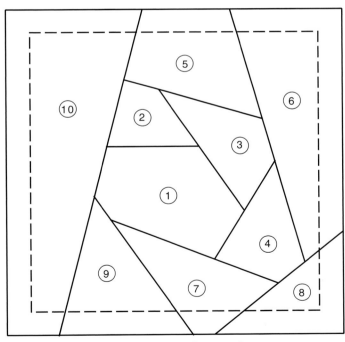

Paper-Piecing Pattern 4

Striped Squares Candle Mat

If you need a small accent mat to place under a candle, vase or other table accessory, try this simple design.

PROJECT SPECIFICATIONS
Skill Level: Beginner
Mat Size: 10⅝" x 10⅝"
Block Size: 3" x 3"
Number of Blocks: 4

FABRIC & BATTING
- Assorted light and dark scraps
- Backing 13" x 13"
- Batting 13" x 13"

SUPPLIES & TOOLS
- Neutral color all-purpose thread
- Quilting thread
- Paper
- Basic tools and supplies

Cutting
1. Sort scraps into light and dark pieces. Cut 10 each light and dark 2⅜" x 2⅜" squares. Cut each square in half on one diagonal to make 22 each light and dark A triangles.

2. Cut remaining scraps into ⅞" x 2¾" strips for pieces 1–6.

Completing the Blocks
1. Make 12 copies of the paper-piecing pattern given.

2. Referring to the instructions for Paper Piecing on page 2 and Figure 1, complete four

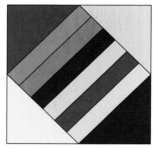

Striped Square
3" x 3" Block

paper-pieced block using the ⅞" x 2¾" strips for pieces 1–6, dark A triangles for pieces 7 and 8 and light A triangles for pieces 9 and 10.

Figure 1

3. Referring to Figure 2, complete partial units, omitting A triangles as necessary; press seams toward A pieces.

Figure 2

Completing the Candle Mat
1. Arrange the whole and partial blocks in rows

with A triangles as shown in Figure 3; join to make rows. Press seams in one direction.

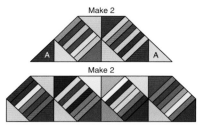

Make 2

Make 2

Figure 3

2. Join the rows to complete the top; press seams in one direction.

3. Remove paper from all paper-pieced blocks.

4. Cut batting and backing pieces the same size as the pieced top using the top as a pattern.

5. Layer the batting, backing right side up and top right side down on the backing; pin to hold.

6. Stitch all around outside edges, leaving a 4" opening on one side; turn right side out through the opening.

7. Press edges flat.

8. Turn the seam allowance at the opening to the inside; press. Hand-stitch to close.

9. Quilt as desired by hand or machine to finish. ■

Scrap of Information
Do you have lots of small triangle scraps? Cut them to size and use as the corner triangles in these blocks.

Striped Squares Candle Mat
Placement Diagram
10⅝" x 10⅝"

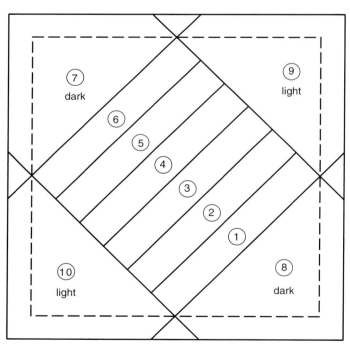

Paper-Piecing Pattern
Make 12 copies

Bow Tie Place Mat

Make a set of two matching place mats to coordinate with any décor using a variety of scraps.

Bow Tie
2½" x 2½" Block

PROJECT SPECIFICATIONS
Skill Level: Beginner
Place Mat Size: 17½" x 12½"
Block Size: 2½" x 2½"
Number of Blocks: 32

FABRIC & BATTING
- Assorted scraps
- ¼ yard white tonal
- ⅓ yard blue mottled
- 2 (19" x 14") backing rectangles
- 2 (19" x 14") batting rectangles

SUPPLIES & TOOLS
- Neutral color all-purpose thread
- Quilting thread
- Template material
- Basic tools and supplies

Cutting
1. Cut two 1¾" x 1¾" B squares and two 1" x 1" D squares from one scrap; repeat for 32 matching B and D sets.

2. Cut three 1¾" by fabric width strips white tonal; subcut strips into (64) 1¾" C squares.

3. Cut one 5½" by fabric width strip blue mottled; subcut strip into two 10½" A rectangles. Cut the remainder of the strip into three 1¾"-wide strips as shown in Figure 1. Subcut these strips into three 15½" F strips, again referring to Figure 1.

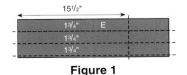

Figure 1

4. Cut two 1¾" by fabric width strips blue mottled; subcut strips into one 15½" E strip and four 13" F strips.

Completing the Blocks
1. Prepare a template for the C/D trimming template using pattern given.

2. Draw a diagonal line from corner to corner on the wrong side of each D square.

3. Referring to Figure 2, place a D square right sides together on one corner of C; stitch on the marked line and trim D seam allowance to ¼". Press D to the right side over the corner of the C square, leaving the C layer in place. Repeat to make 64 C-D units.

Figure 2

4. Use the C/D trimming template to check the size of the C-D units and trim as necessary.

5. Sew a C-D unit to a matching B square as

shown in Figure 3; press seams toward B. Repeat to make 64 B-C-D units.

Figure 3

6. Join two matching B-C-D units to complete one Bow Tie block as shown in Figure 4; press seams in one direction. Repeat to make 32 blocks.

Figure 4

Completing Place Mats

1. To complete one place mat, join four Bow Tie blocks as shown in Figure 5; press seams in one direction. Repeat to make four block strips.

Figure 5

2. Sew a block strip to opposite long sides of A as shown in Figure 6; press seams toward A. Sew the remaining block strips to the remaining sides of A, referring to Placement Diagram; press seams toward A.

Figure 6

3. Sew an E strip to opposite long sides and F strips to the short ends of the pieced center; press seams toward E and F strips to complete one place mat top. Repeat to make two tops.

4. Cut batting and backing pieces the same size as the place mat tops using the top as a pattern.

5. Layer one each batting, backing right side up and top right side down; pin to hold.

6. Stitch all around outside edges, leaving a 4" opening on one side; turn right side out through the opening.

7. Press edges flat.

8. Turn the seam allowance at the opening to the inside; press. Hand-stitch to close.

9. Quilt as desired by hand or machine to finish. Repeat to make two place mats. ■

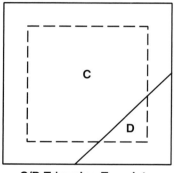

C/D Trimming Template

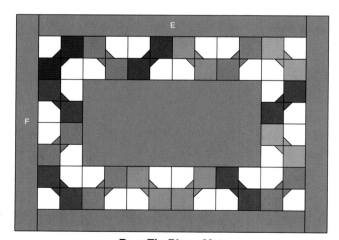

Bow Tie Place Mat
Placement Diagram
17½" x 12½"

Sweet Pea

This scrappy little pink-and-white quilt reminds me of the sweet peas that used to bloom near our back door when I was growing up.

PROJECT SPECIFICATIONS
Skill Level: Beginner
Quilt Size: 12½" x 12½"
Block Size: 1½" x 1½"
Number of Blocks: 64

FABRIC & BATTING
- Scraps pink-with-white prints and white-with-pink prints
- ⅛ yard white solid
- ¼ yard tiny pink-and-white check gingham
- Backing 17" x 17"
- Batting 17" x 17"

SUPPLIES & TOOLS
- Neutral color all-purpose thread
- Quilting thread
- Foundation paper
- Basic sewing tools and supplies

Cutting
1. Cut scraps into 32 each 1¾" x 1¾" white-with-pink A squares and pink-with-white B squares.

2. Cut remaining scraps into 1"-wide strips for white-with-pink C/D and pink-with-white E/F pieces.

3. Cut two ¾" x 12½" G strips and two ¾" x 13" H strips white solid.

4. Cut two 2¼" by fabric width strips tiny pink-and-white check gingham for binding.

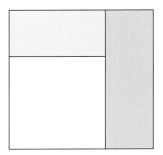

Dark Sweet Pea
1½" x 1½" Block
Make 32

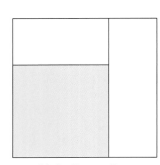

Light Sweet Pea
1½" x 1½" Block
Make 32

Completing the Blocks
1. Make 64 copies of the paper-piecing pattern given.

2. Referring to Paper-Piecing instructions on page 2, complete 32 each Light Sweet Pea and Dark Sweet Pea blocks, referring to the block drawings and Figure 1.

Figure 1

Completing the Top
1. Join two Light Sweet Pea blocks to make a row as shown in Figure 2; press seams to one side. Repeat to make two rows, pressing seams in the second row to the opposite side.

Figure 2

2. Join the two rows to complete a light unit as shown in Figure 3; press seam to one side. Repeat to make eight light units.

Figure 3

3. Repeat steps 1 and 2 to make eight dark units as shown in Figure 4.

Figure 4

4. Join two light units with two dark units to make a row as shown in Figure 5; press seams toward light units. Repeat to make four rows.

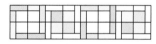

Figure 5

5. Join the rows referring to the Placement Diagram for positioning of units to complete the pieced center; press seams in one direction.

6. Sew a G strip to the top and bottom and H strips to opposite sides of the pieced center to complete the top; press seams toward H and G strips.

7. Remove paper patterns.

8. Complete the quilt referring to Finishing Your Quilt on page 6. ***Note:*** *The sample was machine-quilted around the square centers of the pieced units.* ■

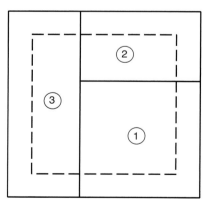

Sweet Pea Paper-Piecing Pattern
Make 64 copies

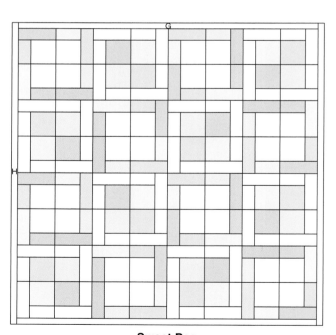

Sweet Pea
Placement Diagram
12½" x 12½"

Floral Trellis Quilt

Use green scraps to form the diagonal trellis and floral scraps to create the garden in this pretty wall quilt.

PROJECT SPECIFICATIONS
Skill Level: Beginner
Quilt Size: 21½" x 21½"
Block Size: 2" x 2"
Number of Blocks: 25

FABRIC & BATTING
- Assorted floral scraps
- 25 (2½" x 2½") A squares green scraps
- ⅛ yard dark green tonal
- ⅝ yard green print
- Backing 27" x 27"
- Batting 27" x 27"

SUPPLIES & TOOLS
- Neutral color all-purpose thread
- Quilting thread
- Template material
- Basic tools and supplies

Cutting
1. Cut (50) 1⅞" x 1⅞" B squares assorted floral scraps.

2. Cut three 1¼" by fabric width strips dark green tonal; subcut strips into two 10½" C strips, two 12" D strips, two 14" G strips and two 15½" H strips.

3. Cut 1½"-wide floral pieces in varying lengths from 2¼"–3" for E and F strips.

4. Cut two 3¾" by fabric width strips green print; subcut each strip into one 15½" I strip and one 22" J strip.

Trellis
2" x 2" Block

5. Cut three 2¼" by fabric width strips green print.

Completing the Blocks
1. Prepare a template for the A/B trimming template using pattern given.

2. Draw a diagonal line from corner to corner on the wrong side of each B square.

3. Referring to Figure 1, place a B square right sides together on one corner of A; stitch on the marked line and trim B seam allowance to ¼". Press B to the right side over the A square corner, leaving the A layer in place. Repeat on the opposite corner of A referring to Figure 2 to complete one Trellis block; repeat to make 25 blocks.

Figure 1 **Figure 2**

4. Use the A/B trimming template to check the size of the blocks and trim as necessary.

Completing the Quilt

1. Join five Trellis blocks to make a row as shown in Figure 3; press seams in one direction. Repeat to make five rows.

Figure 3

2. Join the rows referring to the Placement Diagram to complete the pieced center; press seams in one direction.

3. Sew a C strip to opposite sides and D strips to the top and bottom of the pieced center; press seams toward C and D strips.

4. Join the 1½"-wide strips on short ends to make a 56" long strip; press seams in one direction. Subcut the pieced strip into two 12" E and two 14" F strips.

5. Sew an E strip to opposite sides and F strips to the top and bottom of the pieced center; press seams toward C and D strips.

6. Sew a G strip to opposite sides and H strips to the top and bottom of the pieced center; press seams toward G and H strips.

7. Sew an I strip to opposite sides and J strips to the top and bottom of the pieced center; press seams toward I and J strips to complete the top.

8. Complete the quilt referring to Finishing Your Quilt on page 6. ■

Scrap of Information
Use one green fabric for inner borders to tie the blocks together and make the quilt look less scrappy.

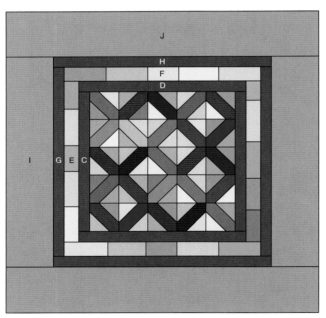

Floral Trellis Quilt
Placement Diagram
21½" x 21½"

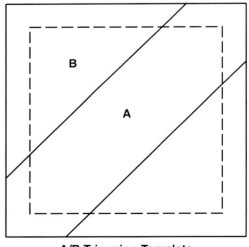

A/B Trimming Template

Striped Triangles Table Mat

Leftover scraps of plaids and stripes are used to make a table mat with a homespun, country look.

PROJECT SPECIFICATIONS
Skill Level: Beginner
Mat Size: 13½" x 13½"
Block Size: 2¼" x 2¼"
Number of Blocks: 24

FABRIC & BATTING
- Assorted light and dark scraps of plaids and stripes
- Backing 16" x 16"
- Batting 16" x 16"

SUPPLIES & TOOLS
- Neutral color all-purpose thread
- Quilting thread
- Paper
- Basic tools and supplies

Cutting
1. Sort scraps into light and dark pieces. Cut the dark scraps into 32 each 1" x 3¼" (piece 1) and 1¼" x 2¾" (piece 2) strips and 2" x 2" (piece 3) squares. Repeat to cut 24 each size from light scraps.

Completing the Blocks
1. Make 28 copies of each of the paper-piecing patterns given.

2. Referring to the instructions for Paper Piecing on page 2 and Figure 1, complete 12 light triangles and 12 reversed light triangles. Repeat

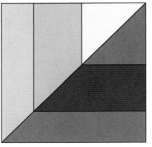
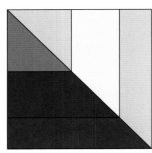

Triangles
2¼" x 2¼" Block
Make 12

Reverse Triangles
2¼" x 2¼" Block
Make 12

to make 16 dark triangles and 16 reversed dark triangles.

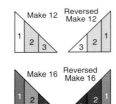

Figure 1

3. Join one reversed light and one dark triangle to make a Triangles block as shown in Figure 2; press seams in one direction. Repeat to make 12 Triangles blocks.

Figure 2

4. Repeat step 3 with a reversed dark triangle and a light triangle to complete a Reverse

HOUSE OF WHITE BIRCHES, BERNE, INDIANA 46711 DRGNETWORK.COM

Triangles block as shown in Figure 3; repeat to make 12 Reverse Triangles blocks. **Note:** *You will have four dark triangles and four reversed dark triangles left.*

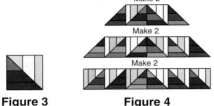

Figure 3   **Figure 4**

Completing the Table Mat

1. Arrange the blocks in rows with the remaining dark triangles and reversed dark triangles as shown in Figure 4. Join in rows; press seams in adjacent rows in opposite directions. Join the rows to complete the pieced top.

2. Remove paper from all paper-pieced blocks.

3. Cut batting and backing pieces the same size as the pieced top using the top as a pattern.

4. Layer the batting, backing right side up and the pieced top right side down on the backing; pin to hold.

5. Stitch all around outside edges, leaving a 4" opening on one side; turn right side out through the opening.

6. Press edges flat.

7. Turn the seam allowance at the opening to the inside; press. Hand-stitch to close.

8. Quilt as desired by hand or machine to finish. ■

Scrap of Information
Remember it is good to have high contrast between the light and dark fabrics. If too many mediums are used, the pattern is lost.

Striped Triangles Table Mat
Placement Diagram
13½" x 13½"

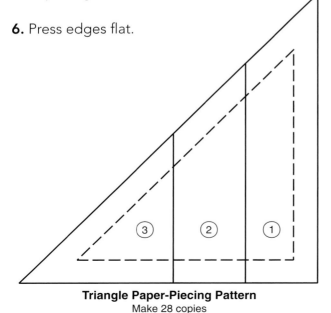

Triangle Paper-Piecing Pattern
Make 28 copies

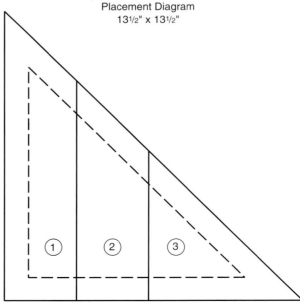

Reverse Triangle Paper-Piecing Pattern
Make 28 copies

Blue Illusions Table Runner

Use blue and white scraps to create this easy-to-stitch table runner.

PROJECT SPECIFICATIONS
Skill Level: Beginner
Runner Size: 22" x 11"
Block Size: 2¾" x 2¾"
Number of Blocks: 10

FABRIC & BATTING
- Assorted blue scraps
- Assorted white and cream scraps
- Backing 24" x 13"
- Batting 24" x 13"

SUPPLIES & TOOLS
- Neutral color all-purpose thread
- Quilting thread
- Paper
- Basic tools and supplies

Cutting
1. Cut blue scraps into 1" (pieces 1 and 2) and 1½" (pieces 5 and 6) widths.

2. Cut white and cream scraps into 1½" widths (pieces 3 and 4).

Completing the Blocks
1. Make copies of the paper-piecing patterns given as directed on patterns.

2. Referring to the instructions for Paper Piecing on page 2 and Figure 1, complete 20 Blue Illusions blocks.

Blue Illusions
2¾" x 2¾" Block

Figure 1   **Figure 2**

3. Repeat step 2 to make eight triangle units referring to Figure 2.

Completing the Table Runner
1. Arrange the pieced blocks and triangle units in rows as shown in Figure 3; join to make rows. Press seams in adjoining rows in opposite directions.

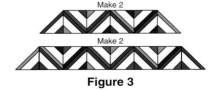

Figure 3

2. Join the rows to complete the top; press seams in one direction.

3. Remove paper from all paper-pieced blocks.

4. Cut batting and backing pieces the same size as the pieced top using the top as a pattern.

5. Layer the batting, backing right side up and top right side down on the backing; pin to hold.

6. Stitch all around outside edges, leaving a 4" opening on one side; turn right side out through the opening.

7. Press edges flat.

8. Turn the seam allowance at the opening to the inside; press. Hand-stitch to close.

9. Quilt as desired by hand or machine to finish. ■

Blue Illusions Table Runner
Placement Diagram
22" x 11"

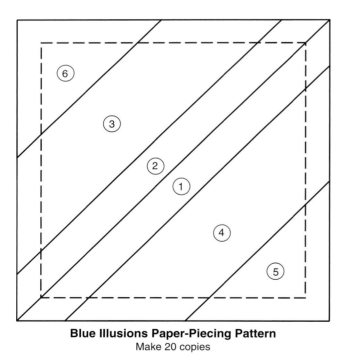

Blue Illusions Paper-Piecing Pattern
Make 20 copies

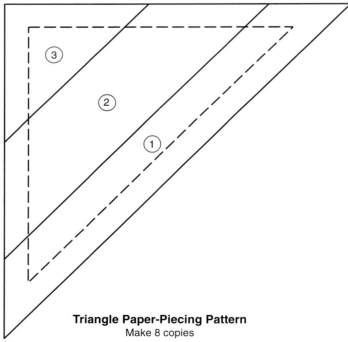

Triangle Paper-Piecing Pattern
Make 8 copies

Stick Pinwheels Place Mat

Use a variety of light scraps as the background for a real scrappy look or use one light-colored fabric for all background pieces for a coordinated look in these easy-to-stitch place mats.

PROJECT SPECIFICATIONS
Skill Level: Beginner
Place Mat Size: 17" x 11¼"
Block Size: 4" x 4"
Number of Blocks: 16

FABRIC & BATTING
Materials make two place mats.
- Assorted green and brown scraps
- ⅜ yard cream tonal
- 2 (19" x 13") backing rectangles
- 2 (19" x 13") batting rectangles

SUPPLIES & TOOLS
- Neutral color all-purpose thread
- Quilting thread
- Paper
- Basic tools and supplies

Cutting
1. Prepare the template for A using pattern given; cut as directed on the piece.

2. Cut three 2½" by fabric width strips cream tonal; subcut strips into (64) 1¾" pieces for piece 1.

3. Cut scraps into 1¾" x 2½" strips for pieces 2, 3 and 4.

Completing the Blocks
1. Make 64 copies of the paper-piecing pattern given.

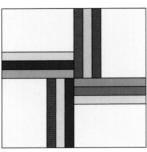

Stick Pinwheel
4" x 4" Block

2. Referring to the instructions for Paper Piecing on page 2 and Figure 1, complete 32 paper-pieced units.

Figure 1   **Figure 2**

3. Join two paper-pieced units to make a row as shown in Figure 2; press seams toward the 4 pieces. Repeat to make two rows.

4. Join the rows to complete one Stick Pinwheel block; press seams in one direction. Repeat for 16 blocks.

Completing the Place Mats
1. Arrange the pieced blocks with the A triangles in diagonal rows as shown in Figure 3; join to

make rows. Press seams toward A and in one direction.

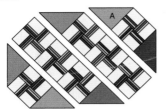

Figure 3

2. Join the rows to complete one place mat top; press seams in one direction. Repeat to make two place mat tops.

3. Remove paper from all paper-pieced blocks.

4. Cut batting and backing pieces the same size as the place mat tops using the top as a pattern.

5. Layer one each batting, backing right side up and top right side down; pin to hold.

6. Stitch all around outside edges, leaving a 4" opening on one side; turn right side out through the opening.

7. Press edges flat.

8. Turn the seam allowance at the opening to the inside; press. Hand-stitch to close.

9. Quilt as desired by hand or machine to finish. Repeat to make two place mats. ■

Scraps of Information
When the same fabric is used for a larger area such as piece 1 in this pattern, it is faster and easier to precut the pieces to fit the paper-pieced foundation.

When the same fabric is used for the background, the quilt does not look as scrappy but the design really shows.

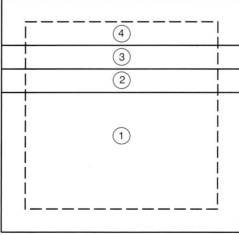

Stick Pinwheels Place Mat
Placement Diagram
17" x 11¼"

Paper-Piecing Pattern
Make 64 copies

A
Cut 6 each green & brown scraps

Mini Logs Wall Quilt

Add small appliquéd flowers to the borders of this tiny Log Cabin–design quilt made with bright scraps.

PROJECT SPECIFICATIONS
Skill Level: Intermediate
Mat Size: 18" x 18"
Block Size: 2" x 2"
Number of Blocks: 25

FABRIC & BATTING
- Assorted bright-color scraps
- 1" x 10½" A strip pink scrap
- 1" x 11" B strip orange scrap
- 1" x 11" C strip blue scrap
- 1" x 11½" D strip green scrap
- ⅛ yard lime green mottled
- ⅛ yard white tonal
- ¼ yard lime green print
- ¼ yard yellow tonal
- Backing 22" x 22"
- Batting 22" x 22"

SUPPLIES & TOOLS
- Neutral color all-purpose thread
- Quilting thread
- Clear monofilament
- Paper
- ⅓ yard fusible web
- 48 small bugle beads
- Basic tools and supplies

Cutting
1. Prepare templates for appliqué shapes using patterns given; trace shapes onto the paper side of the fusible web as directed on each piece for number to cut.

2. Cut out shapes, leaving a margin around each one.

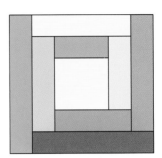

Mini Log Cabin
2" x 2" Block

3. Fuse shapes to the wrong side of fabrics; cut out shapes on traced lines. Remove paper backing.

4. Cut (25) 1¼" x 1¼" squares assorted scraps for piece 1.

5. Cut remaining assorted scraps into ⅞"–1"-wide strips for pieces 2–9.

6. Cut two ¾" by fabric width strips white tonal; subcut strips into two 11½" E strips and two 12" F strips.

7. Cut two 3¾" by fabric width strips yellow tonal; subcut strips into two 12" G strips and two 18½" H strips.

8. Cut three 2¼" by fabric width strips lime green print for binding.

Completing the Blocks
1. Make 25 copies of the paper-piecing pattern given.

2. Referring to the instructions for Paper Piecing